ROALD DAHL

THE WITCHES

MAD LIBS®

by Tristan Roarke

D1037797

MAD LIBS
An Imprint of Penguin Random House LLC, New York

Mad Libs format copyright © 2020 by Penguin Random House LLC.
All rights reserved.

Concept created by Roger Price & Leonard Stern

ROALD DAHL

©2020 The Roald Dahl Story Company Ltd.
ROALD DAHL is a registered trademark of The Roald Dahl Story Company Ltd.
www.roalddahl.com

Illustrations copyright © 1983 by Quentin Blake

Published in 2020 by Mad Libs,
an imprint of Penguin Random House LLC, New York.
Printed in the USA.

Visit us online at www.penguinrandomhouse.com.

ISBN 9780593096482
1 3 5 7 9 10 8 6 4 2

MAD LIBS® is a game for people who don't like games! It can be played by one, two, three, four, or forty.

• RIDICULOUSLY SIMPLE DIRECTIONS

In this tablet you will find stories containing blank spaces where words are left out. One player, the READER, selects one of these stories. The READER does not tell anyone what the story is about. Instead, he/she asks the other players, the WRITERS, to give him/her words. These words are used to fill in the blank spaces in the story.

• TO PLAY

The READER asks each WRITER in turn to call out a word—an adjective or a noun or whatever the space calls for—and uses them to fill in the blank spaces in the story. The result is a MAD LIBS® game.

When the READER then reads the completed MAD LIBS® game to the other players, they will discover that they have written a story that is fantastic, screamingly funny, shocking, silly, crazy, or just plain dumb—depending upon which words each WRITER called out.

• EXAMPLE (*Before* and *After*)

"_____!" he said _____
      EXCLAMATION   ADVERB

as he jumped into his convertible _____ and
           NOUN

drove off with his _____ wife.
      ADJECTIVE

"_____**OUCH**_____!" he said _____**HAPPILY**_____
      EXCLAMATION   ADVERB

as he jumped into his convertible _____**CAT**_____ and
           NOUN

drove off with his _____**BRAVE**_____ wife.
      ADJECTIVE

QUICK REVIEW

In case you have forgotten what adjectives, adverbs, nouns, and verbs are, here is a quick review:

An ADJECTIVE describes something or somebody. *Lumpy, soft, ugly, messy,* and *short* are adjectives.

An ADVERB tells how something is done. It modifies a verb and usually ends in "ly." *Modestly, stupidly, greedily,* and *carefully* are adverbs.

A NOUN is the name of a person, place, or thing. *Sidewalk, umbrella, bridle, bathtub,* and *nose* are nouns.

A VERB is an action word. *Run, pitch, jump,* and *swim* are verbs. Put the verbs in past tense if the directions say PAST TENSE. *Ran, pitched, jumped,* and *swam* are verbs in the past tense.

When we ask for A PLACE, we mean any sort of place: a country or city (*Spain, Cleveland*) or a room (*bathroom, kitchen*).

An EXCLAMATION or SILLY WORD is any sort of funny sound, gasp, grunt, or outcry, like *Wow!, Ouch!, Whomp!, Ick!,* and *Gadzooks!*

When we ask for specific words, like a NUMBER, a COLOR, an ANIMAL, or a PART OF THE BODY, we mean a word that is one of those things, like *seven, blue, horse,* or *head.*

When we ask for a PLURAL, it means more than one. For example, *cat* pluralized is *cats.*

MAD LIBS® is fun to play with friends, but you can also play it by yourself! To begin with, DO NOT look at the story on the page below. Fill in the blanks on this page with the words called for. Then, using the words you have selected, fill in the blank spaces in the story.

Now you've created your own hilarious MAD LIBS® game!

THE WITCHES OF NORWAY

PLURAL NOUN _____

ADJECTIVE _____

VERB ENDING IN "ING" _____

VERB _____

ADJECTIVE _____

VERB ENDING IN "ING" _____

ADJECTIVE _____

NUMBER _____

NOUN _____

COUNTRY _____

PERSON IN ROOM _____

NOUN _____

PLURAL NOUN _____

VERB _____

PLURAL NOUN _____

ADVERB _____

ADJECTIVE _____

OCCUPATION (PLURAL) _____

THE WITCHES OF NORWAY

Norway is a country known for its kind and gentle _____ .

PLURAL NOUN

But did you know that _____ witches are _____

ADJECTIVE VERB ENDING IN "ING"

there, too? _____ it or not, it's _____ . There are

VERB ADJECTIVE

witches hiding in Norway's charming _____ villages

VERB ENDING IN "ING"

and living inside its _____ castles. In fact, some people say

ADJECTIVE

that Norway has over _____ witches! That's probably more than

NUMBER

any other _____ in the world . . . even _____ ! For

NOUN COUNTRY

all you know, _____ may be a witch, or even that sweet

PERSON IN ROOM

old _____ next door! No one knows why so many

NOUN

_____ live in Norway. Maybe it's because their wigs don't

PLURAL NOUN

_____ as much during the long winter _____ .

VERB PLURAL NOUN

Or maybe it's because The Grand High Witch _____ lives

ADVERB

there, too. Whichever is true, one thing is _____ : Norway is

ADJECTIVE

a country of wicked _____ .

OCCUPATION (PLURAL)

From ROALD DAHL: THE WITCHES MAD LIBS® • ©2020 The Roald Dahl Story Company Ltd.
Published by Mad Libs, an imprint of Penguin Random House LLC.

MAD LIBS® is fun to play with friends, but you can also play it by yourself! To begin with, DO NOT look at the story on the page below. Fill in the blanks on this page with the words called for. Then, using the words you have selected, fill in the blank spaces in the story.

Now you've created your own hilarious MAD LIBS® game!

HOW TO SURVIVE A WITCH ENCOUNTER

PLURAL NOUN _____

ADJECTIVE _____

PART OF THE BODY _____

NOUN _____

ANIMAL _____

VERB _____

VERB ENDING IN "S" _____

A PLACE _____

NUMBER _____

NOUN _____

VERB _____

EXCLAMATION _____

CELEBRITY _____

NOUN _____

VERB ENDING IN "ING" _____

PART OF THE BODY _____

VERB _____

Wicked _____ are everywhere! If you're ever unlucky
PLURAL NOUN

enough to encounter one, you must remain _____. Definitely
ADJECTIVE

don't point your _____ at her and shout, "Look! It's a/an
PART OF THE BODY

_____!" If you do that, the witch will catch you and turn
NOUN

you into a tiny _____. If you can, _____ and hide
ANIMAL   VERB

before the witch _____ you. High up in (the)
VERB ENDING IN "S"

_____, under a/an _____-poster bed, or behind a
A PLACE   NUMBER

folding _____ is an excellent place to _____.
NOUN   VERB

If you can't hide, scream, "_____," so someone like
EXCLAMATION

_____ rescues you. If a witch catches you, remember all
CELEBRITY

witches are bald and wear a/an _____ on their head.
NOUN

Try pulling it off and _____ it at the witch's
VERB ENDING IN "ING"

_____. This will make it hard for her to see and hopefully
PART OF THE BODY

give you time to _____!
VERB

From ROALD DAHL: THE WITCHES MAD LIBS® • ©2020 The Roald Dahl Story Company Ltd.
Published by Mad Libs, an imprint of Penguin Random House LLC.

MAD LIBS® is fun to play with friends, but you can also play it by yourself! To begin with, DO NOT look at the story on the page below. Fill in the blanks on this page with the words called for. Then, using the words you have selected, fill in the blank spaces in the story.

Now you've created your own hilarious MAD LIBS® game!

FORMULA 86 DELAYED ACTION MOUSE-MAKER

ADJECTIVE _____

VERB _____

NUMBER _____

NOUN _____

VERB ENDING IN "ING" _____

A PLACE _____

TYPE OF LIQUID _____

ANIMAL _____

ANIMAL _____

VERB _____

PART OF THE BODY _____

NUMBER _____

ADJECTIVE _____

PART OF THE BODY _____

EXCLAMATION _____

OCCUPATION _____

TYPE OF LIQUID _____

VERB ENDING IN "ING" _____

Formula 86 _____ Action Mouse-Maker is very helpful in
　　　　　　　ADJECTIVE

defeating witches, but it's not easy to _____ . After all,
　　　　　　　　　　　　　　　　　VERB

the recipe has over _____ ingredients. The most important
　　　　　　　　　NUMBER

ingredient is the alarm _____ . You can find one
　　　　　　　　　　　NOUN

_____ on the shelf at your local _____ .
VERB ENDING IN "ING"　　　　　　　　　　　　　　A PLACE

You also need to squeeze all the _____ out of a/an
　　　　　　　　　　　　　　TYPE OF LIQUID

_____ . There's even some ingredients no one's ever heard of
ANIMAL

before, like the claw of a/an _____ -cruncher, the snout
　　　　　　　　　　　ANIMAL

of a grobble- _____ , and the _____ of a
　　　　　VERB　　　　　　　　　PART OF THE BODY

blabbersnitch! Making Formula _____ Delayed Action
　　　　　　　　　　　　　NUMBER

Mouse-Maker also requires you to fry forty-five _____
　　　　　　　　　　　　　　　　　　　ADJECTIVE

mice tails in _____ oil. _____ ! Oh, and don't
　　　PART OF THE BODY　　　EXCLAMATION

forget to ask your favorite _____ to help you boil your
　　　　　　　　　OCCUPATION

telescope in hot _____ . That means no more
　　　　　　TYPE OF LIQUID

star- _____ for you!
VERB ENDING IN "ING"

MAD LIBS® is fun to play with friends, but you can also play it by yourself! To begin with, DO NOT look at the story on the page below. Fill in the blanks on this page with the words called for. Then, using the words you have selected, fill in the blank spaces in the story.

Now you've created your own hilarious MAD LIBS® game!

WHAT'S A WITCH TO DO?

NUMBER _____

PERSON IN ROOM _____

PLURAL NOUN _____

VERB _____

ADJECTIVE _____

NOUN _____

PART OF THE BODY _____

PLURAL NOUN _____

FIRST NAME _____

ANIMAL (PLURAL) _____

VERB ENDING IN "ING" _____

PART OF THE BODY (PLURAL) _____

VERB ENDING IN "ING" _____

PART OF THE BODY _____

SILLY WORD _____

ADJECTIVE _____

NOUN _____

ADJECTIVE _____

Witches despise anyone under the age of _____ , like
_____
NUMBER

_____ . To them, clean children smell worse than dogs'
PERSON IN ROOM

_____ . So, they're always trying to think of new ways to
PLURAL NOUN

_____ them. Here's a list of the _____ things witches
VERB   ADJECTIVE

do to children. (Warning: This list will make the _____ on the
NOUN

back of your _____ stand up.)
PART OF THE BODY

- Witches use candy _____ to turn unsuspecting
PLURAL NOUN

  children, like _____ Jenkins, into _____ .
FIRST NAME   ANIMAL (PLURAL)

- Witches like to sing about _____ childrens'
VERB ENDING IN "ING"

  _____ or _____ their
PART OF THE BODY (PLURAL)   VERB ENDING IN "ING"

  _____ . _____ ! That's so _____ !
PART OF THE BODY   SILLY WORD   ADJECTIVE

- Most of all, children who have just taken a warm bubble
  _____ are always turned into something absolutely
  NOUN

  _____ .
  ADJECTIVE

From ROALD DAHL: THE WITCHES MAD LIBS® • ©2020 The Roald Dahl Story Company Ltd.
Published by Mad Libs, an imprint of Penguin Random House LLC.

MAD LIBS® is fun to play with friends, but you can also play it by yourself! To begin with, DO NOT look at the story on the page below. Fill in the blanks on this page with the words called for. Then, using the words you have selected, fill in the blank spaces in the story.

Now you've created your own hilarious MAD LIBS® game!

LEIF THE PORPOISE

NOUN _____

PERSON IN ROOM _____

ANIMAL _____

ADJECTIVE _____

COUNTRY _____

TYPE OF LIQUID _____

ADJECTIVE _____

NOUN _____

SOMETHING ALIVE _____

EXCLAMATION _____

VERB (PAST TENSE) _____

OCCUPATION (PLURAL) _____

PART OF THE BODY _____

NOUN _____

VERB (PAST TENSE) _____

NUMBER _____

OCCUPATION _____

One day, Grandmamma sat in her rocking _____ and told
<u>NOUN</u>

_____ a story. The story was about a boy named Leif who
<u>PERSON IN ROOM</u>

was turned into a/an _____ by some _____ witches
<u>ANIMAL</u> <u>ADJECTIVE</u>

in the waters off the coast of _____ . She said Leif dived
<u>COUNTRY</u>

into the _____ to cool off from the _____
<u>TYPE OF LIQUID</u> <u>ADJECTIVE</u>

summer's day. But when he came up for _____ , he was no
<u>NOUN</u>

longer a/an _____ . Instead, he was a talking porpoise.
<u>SOMETHING ALIVE</u>

"_____ ! I'm a porpoise," cried Leif. His parents
<u>EXCLAMATION</u>

_____ as his brothers and _____
<u>VERB (PAST TENSE)</u> <u>OCCUPATION (PLURAL)</u>

took turns riding on the porpoise by holding onto his slippery

_____ . Then, their beloved _____ just swam away.
<u>PART OF THE BODY</u> <u>NOUN</u>

No one ever discovered why Leif _____ away that day.
<u>VERB (PAST TENSE)</u>

But _____ things are certain . . . Leif was turned into a porpoise
<u>NUMBER</u>

by a/an _____ , and Leif was never heard from again.
<u>OCCUPATION</u>

MAD LIBS® is fun to play with friends, but you can also play it by yourself! To begin with, DO NOT look at the story on the page below. Fill in the blanks on this page with the words called for. Then, using the words you have selected, fill in the blank spaces in the story.

Now you've created your own hilarious MAD LIBS® game!

HOW TO RECOGNIZE A WITCH

ADJECTIVE _____

VERB _____

OCCUPATION _____

VERB _____

ANIMAL (PLURAL) _____

VERB ENDING IN "ING" _____

PART OF THE BODY _____

ADJECTIVE _____

NOUN _____

VERB ENDING IN "ING" _____

TYPE OF LIQUID _____

ANIMAL _____

SILLY WORD _____

NUMBER _____

ADJECTIVE _____

EXCLAMATION _____

ADJECTIVE _____

Can you tell the difference between a witch and a/an _____
                                                          ADJECTIVE

everyday woman? Let's _____ out:
                          VERB

1. You can detect a witch by: (a) taking her to the _____
                                                          OCCUPATION

    for a checkup. Dentists make witches _____ like scaredy-
                                               VERB

    _____ , (b) _____ on her long,
      ANIMAL (PLURAL)   VERB ENDING IN "ING"

    stringy _____ . Witches are _____ as a bowling
              PART OF THE BODY   ADJECTIVE

    _____ , so their hair is always fake.
        NOUN

2. When _____ a child, a witch will: (a) use her
            VERB ENDING IN "ING"

    magic _____ to turn the child into a furry
              TYPE OF LIQUID

    _____ , (b) shout, " _____ " at least _____
        ANIMAL   SILLY WORD   NUMBER

    times.

If you answered *a* for both questions, you're a/an _____ witch
                                                       ADJECTIVE

hunter! If you answered *b* for either question, _____ !
                                                      EXCLAMATION

You're not going to know which woman is a/an _____ witch.
                                                 ADJECTIVE

From ROALD DAHL: THE WITCHES MAD LIBS® • ©2020 The Roald Dahl Story Company Ltd.
Published by Mad Libs, an imprint of Penguin Random House LLC.

MAD LIBS® is fun to play with friends, but you can also play it by yourself! To begin with, DO NOT look at the story on the page below. Fill in the blanks on this page with the words called for. Then, using the words you have selected, fill in the blank spaces in the story.

Now you've created your own hilarious MAD LIBS® game!

INTERVIEW WITH A WITCH

VERB _____

ADJECTIVE _____

PLURAL NOUN _____

VERB _____

SILLY WORD _____

SAME SILLY WORD _____

NUMBER _____

TYPE OF BUILDING _____

PART OF THE BODY (PLURAL) _____

A PLACE _____

NUMBER _____

PLURAL NOUN _____

ANIMAL (PLURAL) _____

EXCLAMATION _____

VERB ENDING IN "ING" _____

VERB (PAST TENSE) _____

ANIMAL _____

THE WITCHES

Interviewer: It's nice to finally _____ a real witch. Tell me,

VERB

why do witches hate cute, _____ _____ so much?

ADJECTIVE _PLURAL NOUN_

Witch: We hate children because they _____ like the worst

VERB

kind of doggy _____ - _____!

SILLY WORD _SAME SILLY WORD_

Interviewer: Really? I have _____ children living in my

NUMBER

_____, and I've never noticed that. Witches must have

TYPE OF BUILDING

very sensitive _____.

PART OF THE BODY (PLURAL)

Witch: Your _____ must smell terrible _____ hours

A PLACE _NUMBER_

a day!

Interviewer: Is there anything you like about little _____?

PLURAL NOUN

Witch: Yes! I like to turn them into pet _____!

ANIMAL (PLURAL)

Interviewer: _____! That's harsh. But thanks for

EXCLAMATION

_____ with me.

VERB ENDING IN "ING"

Witch: I _____ this interview very much. If I didn't,

VERB (PAST TENSE)

I would've turned you into a/an _____.

ANIMAL

From ROALD DAHL: THE WITCHES MAD LIBS® •©2020 The Roald Dahl Story Company Ltd.
Published by Mad Libs, an imprint of Penguin Random House LLC.

MAD LIBS® is fun to play with friends, but you can also play it by yourself! To begin with, DO NOT look at the story on the page below. Fill in the blanks on this page with the words called for. Then, using the words you have selected, fill in the blank spaces in the story.

Now you've created your own hilarious MAD LIBS® game!

PICTURE PERFECT

NOUN _____

CELEBRITY _____

NOUN _____

ADJECTIVE _____

ANIMAL _____

ADJECTIVE _____

ADJECTIVE _____

NOUN _____

VERB _____

VERB _____

NUMBER _____

NOUN _____

NUMBER _____

VERB ENDING IN "ING" _____

PART OF THE BODY _____

NOUN _____

EXCLAMATION _____

MAD LIBS®
PICTURE PERFECT

Hi, my name is Solveg Christiansen. You may know me as the girl who

lives in a framed _____ . I've lived in this painting ever since
                      NOUN

a witch who looked like _____ placed an evil _____
                         CELEBRITY   NOUN

on me. Lucky for me, I ended up in a very _____ painting,
                                            ADJECTIVE

instead of being turned into a/an _____ . The colors here are
                                  ANIMAL

so _____! To be _____ , my _____ hasn't
   ADJECTIVE   ADJECTIVE   NOUN

changed that much since the spell was put on me. I still _____
                                                          VERB

and _____ like a normal girl, although now everything
    VERB

around me is _____-dimensional. One problem with living
             NUMBER

in a painting is that it's surrounded by a wooden _____
                                                   NOUN

on all _____ sides. So, I can't walk very far without
       NUMBER

_____ my _____ on the edge of the
VERB ENDING IN "ING"   PART OF THE BODY

_____ . _____!
NOUN   EXCLAMATION

From ROALD DAHL: THE WITCHES MAD LIBS® • ©2020 The Roald Dahl Story Company Ltd.
Published by Mad Libs, an imprint of Penguin Random House LLC.

MAD LIBS® is fun to play with friends, but you can also play it by yourself! To begin with, DO NOT look at the story on the page below. Fill in the blanks on this page with the words called for. Then, using the words you have selected, fill in the blank spaces in the story.

Now you've created your own hilarious MAD LIBS® game!

WITCH DISGUISES

ADJECTIVE _____

PLURAL NOUN _____

ADJECTIVE _____

A PLACE _____

OCCUPATION (PLURAL) _____

PART OF THE BODY (PLURAL) _____

ARTICLE OF CLOTHING (PLURAL) _____

VERB _____

VERB (PAST TENSE) _____

TYPE OF EVENT _____

NOUN _____

ADJECTIVE _____

VERB _____

VERB ENDING IN "ING" _____

NOUN _____

ADVERB _____

PART OF THE BODY _____

NOUN _____

MAD LIBS

WITCH DISGUISES

Attention, all witches! The _____ High Witch insists that
ADJECTIVE

you wear your full _____ at all times! Looking like

PLURAL NOUN

_____ women who work in the local _____
ADJECTIVE   A PLACE

or who are employed as humble _____ is

OCCUPATION (PLURAL)

critical to our mission. So, no matter how much it hurts your square,

toeless _____ , you must always wear

PART OF THE BODY (PLURAL)

_____ in public. Gloves are also a

ARTICLE OF CLOTHING (PLURAL)

must-_____ and should be _____ to all occasions,
VERB   VERB (PAST TENSE)

even if you're enjoying a long overdue tropical _____ .

TYPE OF EVENT

And if your wig itches like it's made of _____ , that's just too

NOUN

_____ ! You may never _____ it off! After all, you
ADJECTIVE   VERB

never know when a human may be _____ around the

VERB ENDING IN "ING"

next _____ . Finally, and most _____ , keep your
NOUN   ADVERB

mask over your _____ so you can smile! Remember,
PART OF THE BODY

you never get a second chance to make a first _____ .

NOUN

From ROALD DAHL: THE WITCHES MAD LIBS® • ©2020 The Roald Dahl Story Company Ltd.
Published by Mad Libs, an imprint of Penguin Random House LLC.

MAD LIBS® is fun to play with friends, but you can also play it by yourself! To begin with, DO NOT look at the story on the page below. Fill in the blanks on this page with the words called for. Then, using the words you have selected, fill in the blank spaces in the story.

Now you've created your own hilarious MAD LIBS® game!

YOU STINK!

ADJECTIVE _____

VERB _____

VERB ENDING IN "ING" _____

NOUN _____

TYPE OF CONTAINER _____

NOUN _____

TYPE OF FOOD _____

PART OF THE BODY _____

VERB _____

ARTICLE OF CLOTHING (PLURAL) _____

NUMBER _____

ADJECTIVE _____

VERB _____

NOUN _____

VERB _____

NOUN _____

OCCUPATION (PLURAL) _____

THE WITCHES

Witches use their _____ noses to sniff out clean children.
                         ADJECTIVE

Follow these helpful tips to stay dirty so they can't _____ you!
                                                         VERB

1. To stop a witch from _____ you, never use
                              VERB ENDING IN "ING"

   soap when you take a/an _____ or go in the
                                    NOUN

   bath- _____. Instead, roll in _____ or rub
         TYPE OF CONTAINER   NOUN

   a clove of _____ all over your _____ .
                 TYPE OF FOOD   PART OF THE BODY

2. Make sure to always _____ your _____
                            VERB   ARTICLE OF CLOTHING (PLURAL)

   at least _____ times before washing them. Always wear a/an
               NUMBER

   _____ pair of underwear!
       ADJECTIVE

3. Make sure to never _____ your teeth. Otherwise, the
                             VERB

   witches will smell your fresh _____ .
                                        NOUN

   _____ these easy tips and you'll smell as dirty as an old
       VERB

   _____ , and no wicked _____ will be able to
       NOUN   OCCUPATION (PLURAL)

find you!

MAD LIBS® is fun to play with friends, but you can also play it by yourself! To begin with, DO NOT look at the story on the page below. Fill in the blanks on this page with the words called for. Then, using the words you have selected, fill in the blank spaces in the story.

Now you've created your own hilarious MAD LIBS® game!

THE WORST WITCHES

VERB ENDING IN "ING" _____

ADJECTIVE _____

ADJECTIVE _____

ANIMAL (PLURAL) _____

ADJECTIVE _____

PART OF THE BODY _____

ADVERB _____

VERB ENDING IN "ING" _____

ANIMAL (PLURAL) _____

ADVERB _____

VERB ENDING IN "ING" _____

VERB _____

PLURAL NOUN _____

ADJECTIVE _____

VERB ENDING IN "ING" _____

A PLACE _____

VERB _____

ADVERB _____

MAD LIBS
THE WORST WITCHES

Everyone knows that the witches _____ in England
_{VERB ENDING IN "ING"}

are the most _____ witches in the world! These witches are so
_{ADJECTIVE}

horrible because The Grand _____ Witch thinks they're as
_{ADJECTIVE}

lazy as a bunch of _____ . Of course, it doesn't help that
_{ANIMAL (PLURAL)}

the _____ English climate causes their _____ to
_{ADJECTIVE} _{PART OF THE BODY}

itch. They're always _____ _____ their heads
_{ADVERB} _{VERB ENDING IN "ING"}

like they've got _____ living in their wigs. But the main
_{ANIMAL (PLURAL)}

reason English witches behave so _____ is because there are so
_{ADVERB}

many English children _____ outside every day after
_{VERB ENDING IN "ING"}

school. Every time a witch tries to _____ in her home, she
_{VERB}

can't smell anything but sweet English _____ . This makes
_{PLURAL NOUN}

her stomach as _____ as a lemon. So, if you ever find yourself
_{ADJECTIVE}

_____ in (the) _____ and happen to meet
_{VERB ENDING IN "ING"} _{A PLACE}

one of these wicked witches, _____ away as _____
_{VERB} _{ADVERB}

as you can before it's too late!

MAD LIBS® is fun to play with friends, but you can also play it by yourself! To begin with, DO NOT look at the story on the page below. Fill in the blanks on this page with the words called for. Then, using the words you have selected, fill in the blank spaces in the story.

Now you've created your own hilarious MAD LIBS® game!

THE NOT-SO-SWEET SHOP

ADJECTIVE _____

PLURAL NOUN _____

A PLACE _____

TYPE OF FOOD (PLURAL) _____

PLURAL NOUN _____

TYPE OF FOOD (PLURAL) _____

NOUN _____

PLURAL NOUN _____

ADJECTIVE _____

VERB ENDING IN "ING" _____

PLURAL NOUN _____

TYPE OF LIQUID _____

ADJECTIVE _____

EXCLAMATION _____

PLURAL NOUN _____

TYPE OF CONTAINER _____

PART OF THE BODY _____

ANIMAL (PLURAL) _____

Welcome to my sweet shop, you _____ children. Inside the
                                    ADJECTIVE

_____ of this _____ , you'll find the most
PLURAL NOUN   A PLACE

delicious types of _____ for you to enjoy!
                          TYPE OF FOOD (PLURAL)

Everything from chocolate-covered _____ to caramel-filled
                                        PLURAL NOUN

_____ are ready for you to eat. On this side of
TYPE OF FOOD (PLURAL)

the store, we have yummy _____-free sweets with
                              NOUN

_____ sprinkled on top, so grab your favorite and take
PLURAL NOUN

a/an _____ bite! Or try my specialty . . . _____
       ADJECTIVE   VERB ENDING IN "ING"

gooey _____ covered in sticky _____ . Each
         PLURAL NOUN   TYPE OF LIQUID

one of my sweets is made with a/an _____ ingredient that
                                        ADJECTIVE

will make you shout, "_____! This tastes better than a
                          EXCLAMATION

bowl full of _____." But don't be surprised if you wake
                PLURAL NOUN

up being dangled over a/an _____ by your furry
                                TYPE OF CONTAINER

_____ the next morning. My sweets have been known to
PART OF THE BODY

turn children into _____ .
                        ANIMAL (PLURAL)

MAD LIBS® is fun to play with friends, but you can also play it by yourself! To begin with, DO NOT look at the story on the page below. Fill in the blanks on this page with the words called for. Then, using the words you have selected, fill in the blank spaces in the story.

Now you've created your own hilarious MAD LIBS® game!

A WITCHY INVITATION

PLURAL NOUN _____

VERB ENDING IN "ING" _____

VERB (PAST TENSE) _____

NOUN _____

PLURAL NOUN _____

NOUN _____

TYPE OF FOOD _____

NOUN _____

VERB (PAST TENSE) _____

PLURAL NOUN _____

PART OF THE BODY _____

ADJECTIVE _____

COLOR _____

NOUN _____

PLURAL NOUN _____

TYPE OF FOOD _____

MAD LIBS®

A WITCHY INVITATION

In Honor of The Grand High Witch and Her Meeting of

_____ , the Following Shall Be Served for Dinner in the
PLURAL NOUN

_____ Hall:
VERB ENDING IN "ING"

- **Appetizer:** Freshly _____ _____ drizzled
  VERB (PAST TENSE)   NOUN

  with _____ or _____ noodle soup.
       PLURAL NOUN   NOUN

- **Main Course:** Grilled _____ smothered in
                          TYPE OF FOOD

  _____ sauce. Pan- _____ _____
  NOUN   VERB (PAST TENSE)   PLURAL NOUN

  with _____ potatoes. Pasta in a/an _____
       PART OF THE BODY   ADJECTIVE

  sauce sprinkled with crumbled _____ cheese.
                                COLOR

- **Dessert:** Chocolate _____ with raspberry _____
                         NOUN   PLURAL NOUN

  and _____ icing.
      TYPE OF FOOD

MAD LIBS® is fun to play with friends, but you can also play it by yourself! To begin with, DO NOT look at the story on the page below. Fill in the blanks on this page with the words called for. Then, using the words you have selected, fill in the blank spaces in the story.

Now you've created your own hilarious MAD LIBS® game!

SQUEAKY BUSINESS

ANIMAL _____

ADJECTIVE _____

A PLACE _____

NOUN _____

A PLACE _____

SAME TYPE OF ANIMAL _____

VERB _____

VERB _____

NOUN _____

NOUN _____

PART OF THE BODY _____

NOUN _____

EXCLAMATION _____

OCCUPATION (PLURAL) _____

VERB ENDING IN "ING" _____

NOUN _____

LAST NAME _____

So, you want to know what it's like to be turned into a/an _____
ANIMAL

by a witch? You may be surprised, but it's really kinda _____.
ADJECTIVE

When I was a normal kid, I had to go to (the) _____ every day
A PLACE

and learn about boring things like math and _____. Every
NOUN

night I had tons and tons of _____-work. But now that I'm
A PLACE

a/an _____, I can _____ whenever I want, and
SAME TYPE OF ANIMAL   _VERB_

I never have to _____ a book again. I've also got cozy
VERB

_____ covering my body and a long _____ growing
NOUN   _NOUN_

from my _____, which is fun—except when I get it caught
PART OF THE BODY

in a swinging _____. _____! Sometimes I do
NOUN   _EXCLAMATION_

miss talking with my fellow _____ in the schoolyard.
OCCUPATION (PLURAL)

But now my best friend is another _____ mouse who
VERB ENDING IN "ING"

reminds me a lot of my old _____, Bruno _____.
NOUN   _LAST NAME_

MAD LIBS® is fun to play with friends, but you can also play it by yourself! To begin with, DO NOT look at the story on the page below. Fill in the blanks on this page with the words called for. Then, using the words you have selected, fill in the blank spaces in the story.

Now you've created your own hilarious MAD LIBS® game!

WITCH ITCH

ADJECTIVE _____

PART OF THE BODY _____

VERB _____

TYPE OF LIQUID _____

VERB _____

NUMBER _____

TYPE OF FOOD (PLURAL) _____

PLURAL NOUN _____

SAME TYPE OF FOOD (PLURAL) _____

ADJECTIVE _____

TYPE OF CONTAINER _____

PART OF THE BODY _____

NUMBER _____

VERB ENDING IN "ING" _____

NOUN _____

NUMBER _____

PART OF THE BODY _____

ADJECTIVE _____

MAD LIBS

WITCH ITCH

Everyone knows that one of the _____ things about being
                                    ADJECTIVE

a witch is always having an itchy _____. Here's a simple
                                    PART OF THE BODY

recipe you can _____ on your own to end the itch!
                   VERB

1. Take one cup of _____ and _____ it until frothy.
                     TYPE OF LIQUID   VERB

2. Chop _____ _____ into small pieces.
          NUMBER   TYPE OF FOOD (PLURAL)

3. Blend _____ and the _____ until it
           PLURAL NOUN   SAME TYPE OF FOOD (PLURAL)

    looks _____.
           ADJECTIVE

4. Take all the ingredients and mix them in a/an _____.
                                                   TYPE OF CONTAINER

5. Rub the mixture on your _____ and let it sit for
                             PART OF THE BODY

    _____ minutes before _____ it off with a
       NUMBER   VERB ENDING IN "ING"

    warm _____.
          NOUN

If this doesn't work after one application, repeat _____ times
                                                      NUMBER

until your _____ isn't _____ anymore.
            PART OF THE BODY   ADJECTIVE

From ROALD DAHL: THE WITCHES MAD LIBS® • ©2020 The Roald Dahl Story Company Ltd.
Published by Mad Libs, an imprint of Penguin Random House LLC.

MAD LIBS® is fun to play with friends, but you can also play it by yourself! To begin with, DO NOT look at the story on the page below. Fill in the blanks on this page with the words called for. Then, using the words you have selected, fill in the blank spaces in the story.

Now you've created your own hilarious MAD LIBS® game!

THAT STINKS!

PLURAL NOUN _____

ADJECTIVE _____

EXCLAMATION _____

PLURAL NOUN _____

VERB ENDING IN "ING" _____

PLURAL NOUN _____

ADJECTIVE _____

SOMETHING ALIVE _____

ADVERB _____

TYPE OF FOOD _____

TYPE OF LIQUID _____

VERB _____

NOUN _____

PLURAL NOUN _____

PART OF THE BODY _____

VERB ENDING IN "ING" _____

PART OF THE BODY (PLURAL) _____

TYPE OF LIQUID _____

THE WITCHES

MAD LIBS

THAT STINKS!

Witches think human _____ are the smelliest things in the
                          PLURAL NOUN

world! Here is a list of some more _____ things that make
                                          ADJECTIVE

witches scream, "_____!" when they smell them:
                      EXCLAMATION

- Witches think a garden full of _____ smells worse than
                                        PLURAL NOUN

  _____ _____. Few things smell as
  VERB ENDING IN "ING"   PLURAL NOUN

  _____ to a witch as the scent of red _____.
       ADJECTIVE   SOMETHING ALIVE

- The smell of _____ baked _____ covered in
                    ADVERB   TYPE OF FOOD

  _____ sauce will make a witch _____ up.
  TYPE OF LIQUID   VERB

- An expensive French _____ made from freshly picked
                            NOUN

  _____ smells so bad to a witch, her _____
  PLURAL NOUN   PART OF THE BODY

  will start _____ until it falls off.
              VERB ENDING IN "ING"

- Witches really hate the smell of _____. They'd
                                      PART OF THE BODY (PLURAL)

  rather drink a bucket of _____ than have to smell
                              TYPE OF LIQUID

  them!

MAD LIBS® is fun to play with friends, but you can also play it by yourself! To begin with, DO NOT look at the story on the page below. Fill in the blanks on this page with the words called for. Then, using the words you have selected, fill in the blank spaces in the story.

Now you've created your own hilarious MAD LIBS® game!

WITCHES IN TRAINING

ADJECTIVE _____

VERB ENDING IN "ING" _____

ADJECTIVE _____

NUMBER _____

VERB (PAST TENSE) _____

PART OF THE BODY _____

SILLY WORD _____

VERB _____

PLURAL NOUN _____

PLURAL NOUN _____

NOUN _____

NOUN _____

PART OF THE BODY _____

SOMETHING ALIVE _____

NOUN _____

THE WITCHES

By order of The Grand _____ Witch, every witch in
ADJECTIVE

_____ must pass a/an _____ quiz before they
VERB ENDING IN "ING"   ADJECTIVE

can officially be called a witch. You have _____ minutes to
NUMBER

answer the following questions:

1. Every child should be _____ into a mouse because:
    VERB (PAST TENSE)

    (a) their _____ makes an annoying " _____ "
    PART OF THE BODY   SILLY WORD

    noise when they _____ , (b) all _____ smell
    VERB   PLURAL NOUN

    worse than _____ .
    PLURAL NOUN

2. The best way to turn a child into a/an _____ is to: (a) rub
    NOUN

    a blue _____ on their _____ , (b) use
    NOUN   PART OF THE BODY

    Formula 86 Delayed Action _____-Maker to turn
    SOMETHING ALIVE

    them into a mouse.

If you guessed *b* for both questions, congratulations, you're an official

_____ !
NOUN

MAD LIBS® is fun to play with friends, but you can also play it by yourself! To begin with, DO NOT look at the story on the page below. Fill in the blanks on this page with the words called for. Then, using the words you have selected, fill in the blank spaces in the story.

Now you've created your own hilarious MAD LIBS® game!

A WICKED TRANSFORMATION!

ANIMAL _____

ADJECTIVE _____

PART OF THE BODY _____

PART OF THE BODY (PLURAL) _____

VERB _____

COLOR _____

ADJECTIVE _____

PLURAL NOUN _____

PART OF THE BODY (PLURAL) _____

VERB ENDING IN "ING" _____

ADJECTIVE _____

VERB _____

PART OF THE BODY _____

PLURAL NOUN _____

ADJECTIVE _____

TYPE OF FOOD _____

THE WITCHES

MAD LIBS
A WICKED TRANSFORMATION!

If a witch ever turns you into a/an _____ , the first thing

_____ANIMAL_____

you'll notice is a/an _____ feeling in your _____ .

_____ADJECTIVE_____PART OF THE BODY

Next, your _____ will start to _____ , and

_____PART OF THE BODY (PLURAL)_____VERB_____

all the _____ teeth in your mouth will become really

_____COLOR_____

_____ . Then, brown _____ will start to grow all

ADJECTIVE_____PLURAL NOUN

over your _____ until you're completely covered.

_____PART OF THE BODY (PLURAL)_____

In the last stages, your voice will start _____ like a

_____VERB ENDING IN "ING"

mouse, and _____ whiskers will _____ out of your

_____ADJECTIVE_____VERB_____

_____ . Finally, your fingers and toes will turn into

_____PART OF THE BODY_____

_____ . But don't be too _____ . The good news

PLURAL NOUN_____ADJECTIVE

is that now you'll get to eat all the swiss _____ you want!

_____TYPE OF FOOD

From ROALD DAHL: THE WITCHES MAD LIBS® • ©2020 The Roald Dahl Story Company Ltd.
Published by Mad Libs, an imprint of Penguin Random House LLC.

MAD LIBS® is fun to play with friends, but you can also play it by yourself! To begin with, DO NOT look at the story on the page below. Fill in the blanks on this page with the words called for. Then, using the words you have selected, fill in the blank spaces in the story.

Now you've created your own hilarious MAD LIBS® game!

INTERVIEW WITH
THE GRAND HIGH WITCH

VERB _____

NOUN _____

PLURAL NOUN _____

ADVERB _____

NOUN _____

ADJECTIVE _____

ADJECTIVE _____

NUMBER _____

PLURAL NOUN _____

EXCLAMATION _____

PLURAL NOUN _____

PART OF THE BODY (PLURAL) _____

ADJECTIVE _____

VERB ENDING IN "ING" _____

TYPE OF FOOD _____

NOUN _____

ANIMAL _____

THE WITCHES

MAD LIBS
INTERVIEW WITH
THE GRAND HIGH WITCH

Student: Thank you for letting me _____ you for an article
<u>VERB</u>

in my school _____ about _____ .
<u>NOUN</u> <u>PLURAL NOUN</u>

The Grand High Witch: Let's get this over vith as _____ as
<u>ADVERB</u>

possible! You smell more disgusting than a/an _____ on a/an
<u>NOUN</u>

_____ summer's day!
<u>ADJECTIVE</u>

Student: How did you become The _____ High Witch?
<u>ADJECTIVE</u>

The Grand High Witch: _____ years ago, I gathered all the
<u>NUMBER</u>

other _____ in Norvay. I cast a spell by shouting,
<u>PLURAL NOUN</u>

"_____!" and shooting _____ from my
<u>EXCLAMATION</u> <u>PLURAL NOUN</u>

_____ . The other vitches vere very _____ .
<u>PART OF THE BODY (PLURAL)</u> <u>ADJECTIVE</u>

Also, I have a magic money- _____ machine. Vould
<u>VERB ENDING IN "ING"</u>

you like a piece of _____ ?
<u>TYPE OF FOOD</u>

Student: Um . . . no thank you! I think this _____ is over!
<u>NOUN</u>

The Grand High Witch: Too bad. You vould have made a nice

_____ for my collection.
<u>ANIMAL</u>

MAD LIBS® is fun to play with friends, but you can also play it by yourself! To begin with, DO NOT look at the story on the page below. Fill in the blanks on this page with the words called for. Then, using the words you have selected, fill in the blank spaces in the story.

Now you've created your own hilarious MAD LIBS® game!

FROG VLOG!

CELEBRITY _____

ADJECTIVE _____

OCCUPATION _____

ANIMAL _____

VERB (PAST TENSE) _____

VERB (PAST TENSE) _____

ADJECTIVE _____

NOUN _____

PART OF THE BODY (PLURAL) _____

TYPE OF CONTAINER (PLURAL) _____

LETTER OF THE ALPHABET _____

VERB _____

ADVERB _____

VERB (PAST TENSE) _____

EXCLAMATION _____

NOUN _____

VERB ENDING IN "ING" _____

NOUN _____

THE WITCHES

MAD LIBS

FROG VLOG!

Hi and ribbit! It's me, _____! I know I look like a frog and
　　　　　　　　　　　　CELEBRITY

not a/an _____ internet personality, but that's because The
　　　　　　ADJECTIVE

Grand High _____ turned me into a/an _____.
　　　　　　　OCCUPATION　　　　　　　　　　　　　　　ANIMAL

Anyway, let's hop to it! In today's video, I want to tell you about a

mouse that _____ into The Grand High Witch's hotel
　　　　　　VERB (PAST TENSE)

room to steal Formula 86 _____ Action Mouse-
　　　　　　　　　　　　　VERB (PAST TENSE)

Maker. It was _____! He found the potion hidden inside
　　　　　　　ADJECTIVE

the _____ on the witch's bed and had to tear apart
　　　NOUN

the mattress with his tiny _____ to get the
　　　　　　　　　　　　　PART OF THE BODY (PLURAL)

_____ of formula out. But then, the big
TYPE OF CONTAINER (PLURAL)

G-_____-W came into the room. I was certain she
　　LETTER OF THE ALPHABET

was going to _____ him! _____, he was able to
　　　　　　　VERB　　　　　　　　ADVERB

escape when some other witches _____ the door.
　　　　　　　　　　　　　　　　VERB (PAST TENSE)

_____! What an exciting _____! Thanks for
EXCLAMATION　　　　　　　　　　　　　NOUN

_____! Don't forget to hit the subscribe _____
VERB ENDING IN "ING"　　　　　　　　　　　　　　　　　　NOUN

for more fun, froggy videos!

MAD LIBS® is fun to play with friends, but you can also play it by yourself! To begin with, DO NOT look at the story on the page below. Fill in the blanks on this page with the words called for. Then, using the words you have selected, fill in the blank spaces in the story.

Now you've created your own hilarious MAD LIBS® game!

GOODBYE, WITCHES!

ADJECTIVE _____

VERB _____

VERB _____

VERB ENDING IN "ING" _____

TYPE OF LIQUID _____

SILLY WORD _____

VERB ENDING IN "S" _____

ADJECTIVE _____

TYPE OF FOOD _____

TYPE OF EVENT _____

NUMBER _____

NOUN _____

PLURAL NOUN _____

VERB _____

ADJECTIVE _____

VERB ENDING IN "ING" _____

NOUN _____

PLURAL NOUN _____

THE WITCHES

MAD LIBS

GOODBYE, WITCHES!

Grandmamma here. Since witches are such _____ creatures,
                                          ADJECTIVE

I've made it my lifelong goal to _____ every last witch on
                                      VERB

the planet! One of my grandson's favorite ways to _____ a
                                                       VERB

witch is to trick her into _____ her own magic
                            VERB ENDING IN "ING"

_____. There's nothing we enjoy more than hearing a
TYPE OF LIQUID

witch shriek, " _____," before she _____
                  SILLY WORD   VERB ENDING IN "S"

forever. The best way to get a witch to drink her own formula is to pour

it into some _____ _____ during the witches'
                ADJECTIVE   TYPE OF FOOD

Annual _____. After that, it's as easy as one, two,
         TYPE OF EVENT

_____! Before you know it, that bottle of Formula 86 Delayed
  NUMBER

Action _____-Maker will turn all those witches into furry
         NOUN

_____! Just make sure to _____ the _____
PLURAL NOUN   VERB   ADJECTIVE

creature after she transforms by _____ her in a/an
                                   VERB ENDING IN "ING"

_____. That will ensure she never scares any sweet little
NOUN

_____ again!
PLURAL NOUN

From ROALD DAHL: THE WITCHES MAD LIBS® • ©2020 The Roald Dahl Story Company Ltd.
Published by Mad Libs, an imprint of Penguin Random House LLC.

Download Mad Libs today!

stories on our apps!

creating wacky and wonderful

Join the millions of Mad Libs fans